Brazilian Bossa Novas with Jim

Bob Zottola, *Trumpet*

Also suitable for any B♭ instrument: Trumpet,
Flugelhorn, Clarinet, Tenor Sax, Soprano Sax

PLAYBACK+
Speed • Pitch • Balance • Loop

To access audio, visit:
www.halleonard.com/mylibrary
Enter Code
6854-6238-1568-1673

ISBN 978-1-59615-820-7

EXCLUSIVELY DISTRIBUTED BY
HAL•LEONARD®

Visit Hal Leonard Online at
www.halleonard.com

World headquarters, contact:
Hal Leonard
7777 West Bluemound Road
Milwaukee, WI 53213
Email: info@halleonard.com

In Europe, contact:
Hal Leonard Europe Limited
1 Red Place
London, W1K 6PL
Email: info@halleonardeurope.com

In Australia, contact:
Hal Leonard Australia Pty. Ltd.
4 Lentara Court
Cheltenham, Victoria, 3192 Australia
Email: info@halleonard.com.au

CONTENTS

THE GIRL FROM IPANEMA

Bb TRUMPET (FLUGELHORN)

Music by Antonio Carlos Jobim

THE GIRL FROM IPANEMA

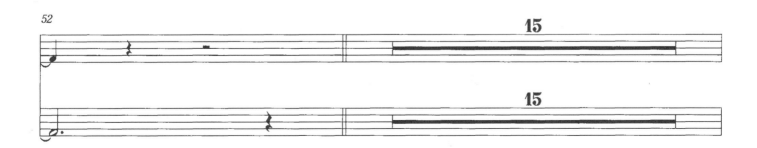

THE GIRL FROM IPANEMA

SO DANÇO SAMBA

(Jazz 'n' Samba)

Bb TRUMPET (FLUGELHORN)

Music by Antonio Carlos Jobim

SO DANÇO SAMBA

SO DANÇO SAMBA

ONCE I LOVED

Bb TRUMPET (FLUGELHORN)

Music by Antonio Carlos Jobim

ONCE I LOVED

ONCE I LOVED

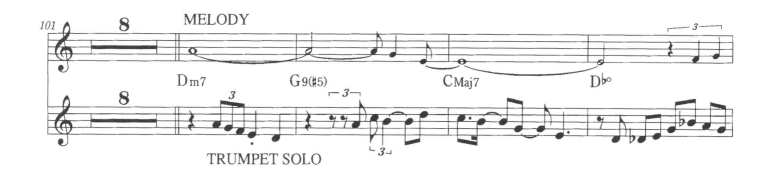

MELODY

TRUMPET SOLO

ONCE I LOVED

DINDI

Bb TRUMPET (FLUGELHORN)

Music by Antonio Carlos Jobim

DINDI

This page has been intentionally left blank to facilitate page turns.

ONE NOTE SAMBA

Bb TRUMPET (FLUGELHORN)

Music by Antonio Carlos Jobim

ONE NOTE SAMBA

ONE NOTE SAMBA

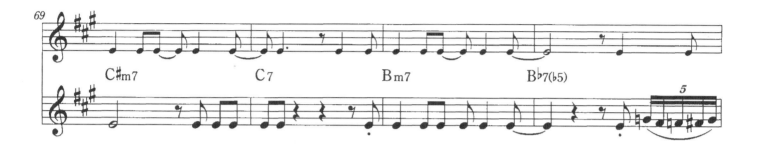

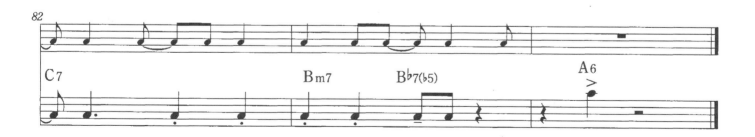

MEDITATION

Bb TRUMPET (FLUGELHORN)

Music by Antonio Carlos Jobim

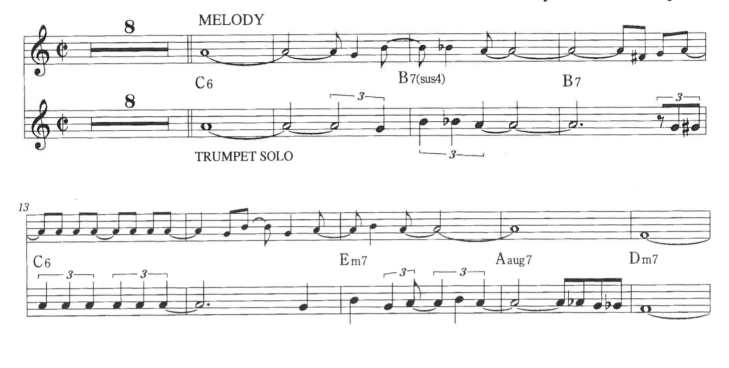

MEDITATION

HOW INSENSITIVE

Bb TRUMPET (FLUGELHORN)

Music by Antonio Carlos Jobim

HOW INSENSITIVE

TRISTE

Bb TRUMPET (FLUGELHORN)

Music by Antonio Carlos Jobim

TRISTE

TRISTE

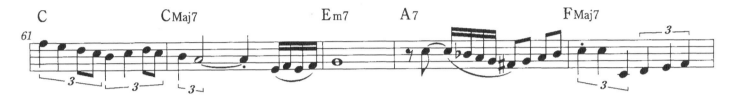

NOTE:

IS OFTEN PLAYED AS:

This page has been intentionally left blank to facilitate page turns.

CORCOVADO
(Quiet Nights of Quiet Stars)

Bb TRUMPET (FLUGELHORN)

Music by Antonio Carlos Jobim

CORCOVADO

WAVE

Bb TRUMPET (FLUGELHORN)

Music by Antonio Carlos Jobim

WAVE

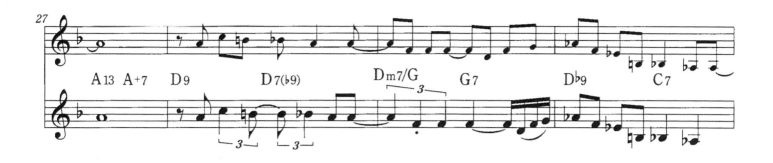

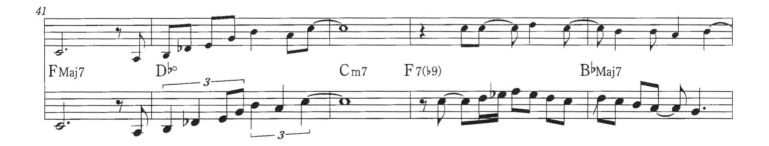

WAVE